Women in Islam

What the Qur'an and Sunnah Say

────── ༄ ──────

Abdur Raheem Kidwai

KUBE
PUBLISHING

Women in Islam: *What the Qur'an and Sunnah Say*

First Published in England by
Kube Publishing Ltd
Markfield Conference Centre
Ratby Lane, Markfield
Leicestershire, LE67 9SY
United Kingdom
t: +44 (0) 1530 249230
e: info@kubepublishing.com

www.kubepublishing.com

Cataloguing-in-Publication Data is available from the
British Library

ISBN: 978-1-84774-140-0 Casebound
ISBN: 978-1-84774-149-3 ebook

Cover Design: Jannah Haque
Interior Design & Typesetting: Imtiaze Ahmed
Printed by: Elma Basim, Turkey.

Contents

iii

>> >>

In the name of Allah, Most Compassionate, Most Merciful

Preface

Increasingly, certain Islamic practices have been isolated as imposing degradation and suffering upon women. Within the comprehensive framework that Islam aims to establish individually and collectively; aspects of the faith such as polygamy, divorce, patriarchy, segregation of the sexes etc. cannot be overlooked. However, taking them in isolation does not allow a full appreciation of the kind of equality, dignity and exalted status that the Qur'an and Hadith accord women, especially as a mother, wife and daughter.

Some socio-cultural practices in Muslim societies, past and present, that have become the norm – cannot and should not befog the Islamic stance on women. This work provides readers with an opportunity to consider some of the references to women in authentic Islamic sources in order to shape an informed view.

Specifically, *Women in Islam* aims to let readers appreciate the high status that women enjoy in Islam. Needless to say, Islam confirms that women and men are different; yet these differences are

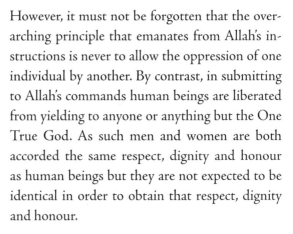

valued and given respect as facets of how Allah has created human beings. To be equal in the sight of Allah a woman does not need to be the same as a man; she does not need to compete nor compare herself to a man because the 'male' of the human species is not the standard by which Allah judges. Differences exist yet both are made to complement each other and to work together; neither is superior nor inferior to the other.

Without a doubt, men and women have distinct commands that apply to them; they have specific responsibilities and clear rights, regardless of which, Allah's justice is evident in all His directives. Islam, as a way of life, recognises that everyone does not play the same role in society and thus for any collective to operate specific guidelines are required.

However, it must not be forgotten that the overarching principle that emanates from Allah's instructions is never to allow the oppression of one individual by another. By contrast, in submitting to Allah's commands human beings are liberated from yielding to anyone or anything but the One True God. As such men and women are both accorded the same respect, dignity and honour as human beings but they are not expected to be identical in order to obtain that respect, dignity and honour.

In this book, passages from the Qur'an and Hadith collections have been cited that reflect the Islamic stance on womanhood: her existence as a creation of Allah, her purpose of life as a slave of Allah, her capacity for attaining self-development and proximity with Allah and her accomplishments. Together with men they are addressed and urged to be active, positive stakeholders in the construction of a God-conscious society and for attaining salvation as pious individuals who are obedient to Allah.

Both believing men and women are promised all the bounties of Paradise and eternal success and happiness in the Next World and are held as equally responsible for their actions and conduct. In order to illustrate this point, specific narratives of women mentioned in the Qur'an, both role models and examples of those who did wrong, have been included.

With a view to exemplify the dynamic contribution that Muslim women have made to Islamic society prominent Hadith scholars from early Muslim history have also been noted.

I am grateful to Br. Haris Ahmad and Br. Yahya Birt for entrusting this assignment to me. Kube Publishing has made a mark over the years as a leading publisher of books on Islam and Muslims.

I must thank the Kube Publishing team for the high standard of production. I benefitted much from a discerning reading of this work in its manuscript form by my wife, Sarah and my worthy colleague, Dr. Faiza Abbasi, Aligarh Muslim University, Aligarh, India

I look forward to suggestions for improving this work in its next edition.

Abdur Raheem Kidwai

Aligarh, India, July 2020

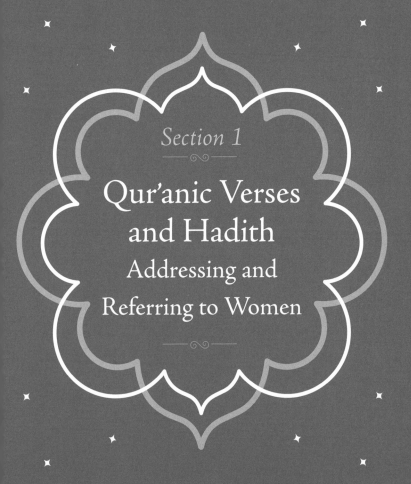

Section 1

Qur'anic Verses
and Hadith
Addressing and
Referring to Women

THE BELIEVERS, men and women, are protectors one of another: they enjoin what is just, and forbid what is evil; they observe regular prayers, practice regular charity, and obey Allah and His Messenger. On them will Allah pour His mercy: for Allah is Exalted in power, Wise.

Allah has promised to believers, men and women, Gardens under which rivers flow, to dwell therein, and beautiful mansions in Gardens of everlasting bliss. But the greatest bliss is the good pleasure of Allah: that is the supreme felicity.

(AL-TAWBAH 9: 71-72)

Islam perceives men and women as sincere friends and soulmates to each other. The above passage promises the same, equal reward to the believing men and women who do good.

2

Whoever does good – man or woman and is a believer – Allah will grant them a good life. He will certainly reward them for their good actions.

(AL-NAHL 16: 97)

3

Allah promises forgiveness and a great reward to:
- the men and women who have faith,
- the men and women who are obedient,
- the men and women who are truthful,
- the men and women who are patient,
- the men and women who humble themselves before Allah,
- the men and women who give in charity,
- the men and women who fast,
- the men and women who guard their chastity, and
- the men and women who remember Allah much.

(AL-AHZAB 33: 35)

This is a comprehensive profile of those, men and women alike, who will win Allah's pleasure.
The Qur'an makes no distinction between men and women in having faith, being truthful and doing good; including being chaste. Honour and chastity are requirements of the conduct of both women and men, obligations excluding neither one nor the other.

4

Allah will admit the believing men and women to the Gardens (*Jannah*) beneath which rivers flow. They will live there. He will remove their sins. With Allah is great success.

(AL-FATH 48: 5)

The doors of Allah's mercy and forgiveness and of Paradise are wide open, equally, for both men and women.

5

Do not be jealous over what God has given more to some than others. Men will get a share for what they do and women will get a share for what they do.

(AL-NISA' 4: 32)

The Qur'an is clear in pointing out that men and women will be recompensed alike; there is no distinction between men and women.

6

O believers, let not some men among you laugh at others. It may be that the others are better. Let not some women laugh at others. It may be that the others are better. Do not defame one another. Do not taunt one another by (offensive) nick-names. After having faith, it is bad to commit any sin. Those who do not repent are wrong-doers.

(AL-HUJURAT 49: 11)

In Islam an identical moral code applies to both men and women. According to the Qur'an, it is unbecoming; rather, unthinkable for a believing man or woman to commit any act which may destroy the fabric of an inclusive and peaceful society, which all Muslim men and women are obliged to maintain. The above Qur'anic advice aims at promoting and protecting social relations.

On the Day of Judgement, you will see the believing men and women – how their light will run before them and on their right hand. (They will be told:) 'Good news for you today! There are Gardens for you beneath which rivers flow. You will live in these. This is a great success.'

(al-Hadid 57: 12)

'O my Lord, forgive me, my parents, and every believer who enters my house. Forgive all believing men and women.'

(Nuh 71: 28)

❋

This Qur'anic supplication highlights the importance of asking for forgiveness, for men and women alike. The specification made evident here in the mention of parents, then believers entering the home, then man

8

kind; suggests that Allah is instructing us to make a conscious effort to extend our dua of forgiveness to all believing men and women, not just those in our immediate circle of friends. This creates a mindset of concern for oneself and the ummah, combining individual and collective success in this life and the next.

Seek God's pardon for your faults and for the believing men and women.

(MUHAMMAD 47:19)

9

If those men and women who give in charity give a good loan to Allah, it will be increased manifold for them. There is honourable reward for them.

(al-Hadid 57: 18)

✻

Women, like men, are advised to strike this deal with Allah, which assures immense profit for them. This Qur'anic passage assumes that women, like men, have the means to give in charity; for in Islam women have economic independence to manage their wealth and decide how to use it appropriately.

11

O Prophet, tell your wives and daughters, and the believing women to draw a part of their outer garments around them. This is so that they be recognised and be not molested. Allah is Most Forgiving, Most Merciful.

(AL-AHZAB 33: 59)

✳

The protection and dignity of women permeates this Qur'anic directive for their modest dress.

11

∽ 12 ∾

It is one of Allah's signs that He created for you mates from your own kind so that you may find comfort in them. He has put love and mercy between you (man and wife). In this are signs for those who reflect.

(AL-RUM 30: 21)

❈

A Qur'anic passage underscoring the basic bond of love and kindness between men and women. Allah has enjoined marriage to be a relationship where both spouses are responsible for being a source of comfort and support to each other.

Allah's is the kingdom of the heavens and the earth. He creates what He wills. He grants females to whom He wills and males to whom He wills. Or He grants them both males and females. He leaves childless whom He wills. He is All Knowing, All Powerful.

(AL-SHURA 42: 49–50)

Having a daughter or son or both or neither is all part of the Divine decree. Both daughters and sons are Allah's gifts, for which we should be grateful to Him. Likewise, being childless is not a curse, as is mistakenly held by some. This Qur'anic passage declares that the bestowal of sons or daughters or otherwise is Allah's decision which we should accept gracefully and humbly.

13

O people, Allah has created you from
a male and a female. He has made you
into communities and tribes so that you
may recognise one another. The most
honourable one among you in the sight
of Allah is the one who fears Him most.
Allah is All Knowing, All Aware.

(al-Hujurat 49: 13)

*This ayah makes a point of mentioning men and
women and then goes on to highlight how communities
and tribes have come about from the basic building
block of a man and a woman, but the thing that
is important in the sight of Allah is a person's God-
consciousness; not their gender, race or nationality.
The more pious a man or woman is, the closer he or
she is to Allah, which is the highest felicity imaginable.*

∽ 15 ∽

Do not even go near sex outside marriage.
It is shameful and an evil path.

(AL-ISRA' 17: 32)

※

*This Qur'anic statement makes no distinction between
a man or a woman in the application of this directive.
It points to the devastating effects of sexual misconduct
on both the individual's soul and on society at large.
It is common knowledge that sexual crimes destroy
the social fabric and hence the Qur'anic caution:
Do not even draw near to any sexual misconduct, let
alone committing any unlawful sexual act.*

Those guilty of sex outside marriage, be they male or female; flog each one of them with one hundred whips. Let not mercy move you in their case. For this is about Allah's religion, if you believe in Allah and the Last Day. Let a group of believers witness their punishment.

(AL-NUR 24: 2)

In Islam, those guilty of sexual misconduct, be they men or women, receive the same punishment. In the interest of establishing a harmonious social order Islam takes a very serious view of sexual crimes and prescribes the above deterrent punishment.

~ 17 ~

Allah has given you mates of your own kind. He has granted you through your mates children and grandchildren. He gives you pure and wholesome things to eat. Do people still believe in falsehood and disbelieve in Allah's signs?

(AL-NAHL 16: 72)

※

Spouses, children and food are listed here as Allah's great bounties, all of which we should appreciate; we should be thankful to Allah for them. The above Qur'anic passage also underscores the perfect compatibility between a man and a woman. Being created from the same kind, they are made for each other.

~ 18 ~

This is a message (full of advice and lessons).
There is an excellent end for the pious.
The gates of the eternal gardens of Paradise
will be wide open for them. They will
sit there and ask for fruits and drinks in
plenty. With them there will be chaste
women of the same age.

(SAD 38: 49-52)

18

*This ayah mentions the company of chaste women as
one of the bounties of Paradise, although the audi-
ence here is men, it highlights the value of chastity
in Islam. Chastity is a prized blessing, something to
aspire to and appreciate in this life since it receives
mention as one of the blessings of Paradise.*

(It will be said to them:) 'O My servants, have no fear or grief on this Day (of Judgement).' For they believed in Allah's signs and were Muslims. (It will be said:) 'Enter Paradise, you and your wives, full of joy.'

(al-Zukhruf 43: 68-70)

❋

To gain entry into Paradise is a reward that we want for ourselves and our loved ones, Allah promises pious men and their wives this reward. Muslims will have all the joys of family life in Paradise.

Allah will unite the believers with their believing children. He will not deny them any reward for their good actions. Everyone is responsible, as on an oath, for their actions.

(AL-TUR 52: 21)

The believers, be they men or women, will enjoy the company of their believing children in Paradise. It is therefore the duty of parents to ensure that their children grow up as believers, instilling values and virtues in them that will bring them success in both worlds.

20

~ 21 ~

Can the reward for good be anything except good?

(AL-RAHMAN 55: 60)

*

This Divine promise of reward is for everyone, irrespective of gender, caste, colour, nationality or any other label. Allah has promised His reward for all those who do good while taking Allah, the One True God, as their Lord.

They (the believers) will sit, facing one another (in Paradise).

Ever-young youth will go around them, serving them with cups filled with drinks from a clear spring.

(AL-WAQI'AH 56: 16-18)

Elsewhere in the Qur'an, houris (beautiful damsels) are mentioned. Here the image has been expanded and ever-young youth are referred to as another joy of Paradise. This is a measure of the sensitivity portrayed in the Qur'an. Like men, women will also have beautiful, young companions.

22

~ 23 ~

Ever-young youth will serve them (the believers in Paradise). When you see these youth, you would think that they are scattered pearls. When you will look around, you see all-round bliss and the glory of a great kingdom.

(AL-DAHR 76: 19-20)

❋

The charms of these ever-young youth in Paradise are mentioned almost in the same terms in which the beauty of houris (damsels) in Paradise is described in the Qur'an.

23

When the good news of (the birth) of a daughter is given to any of them, his face turns black. He is filled with anger and sorrow.

He hides himself from people because of the bad news. Should he retain her and face humiliation or bury her? What an evil choice to make!

(AL-NAHL 16: 58–59)

❋

The Qur'an condemns in very strong terms the barbaric Arab Jahiliyyah (pre-Islamic) practice of burying daughters alive. In Islam, sons and daughters are alike, representing as they do Allah's gift to humankind. Several Hadith highlight the excellence of bringing up a daughter.

25

When (on the Day of Judgement) the girl-child buried alive will be asked — for what crime was she killed

(AL-TAKWIR 81: 8-9)

✳

The Qur'an denounced the pre-Islamic Arab practice of burying daughters alive. Those guilty of it will receive severe punishment in the Hereafter.
The egalitarian teachings that prevailed with the spread of Islam sought to end this barbaric practice.

25

∽ 26 ∽

There is a share for men in what their parents and close relatives leave behind. Likewise, there is a share for women in what their parents and close relatives leave behind. The share is decided by Allah in what is left behind, be it little or much.

(AL-NISA' 4: 7)

※

The Islamic law of inheritance, recognises both women and men as inheritors; it broke the norm prevalent at the time whereby women themselves were inherited like a possession and did not have an identity of their own. Accordingly, men and women as heirs are mentioned in these two separate verses in an identical manner.

(O Prophet), people ask you the ruling. Say: 'God commands you about the inheritance of him who does not leave behind any heir in direct line.

If a man dies childless, but has a sister she will have half the inheritance… if there are two sisters, they shall have two-thirds of the inheritance. If there are brothers and sisters, the male shall have the share of two females.'

(AL-NISA' 4: 176)

Islam does not place the financial responsibility on women; it is the duty of the father, brother, husband and son to support a woman. Despite this she has a share in inheritance as a mother, sister, wife and daughter.

They ask you about menstruation. Say: 'It is a state of impurity.' So, keep away from women in the state of impurity. Do not approach them sexually until they are clean. Approach them sexually when they are clean in the manner prescribed by Allah for you. Allah loves those who turn to Him in repentance. He loves those who keep themselves pure and clean.

(AL-BAQARAH 2: 222)

The Qur'an refers to menstruation as a brief, temporary period of impurity, during which sexual relations are to be stopped. Far from branding menstruation as 'God's curse' or the 'Curse of Eve', the Qur'an implies it is a natural part of a woman's life.

∾ 29 ∾

Allah instructs man to be good to his parents. His mother gives him birth with much pain. Then his weaning lasts for two years. So thank your parents. To Allah is everyone's return.

(LUQMAN 31: 14)

A special mention is made of the hardship suffered by a mother – in giving birth and in feeding a child. Accordingly, in Islam, she is entitled to more love and respect. The following Hadith further illustrates the point:

i. *Prophet Muhammad (peace be upon him) pointed out: 'Paradise lies at the feet of your mother.'*
ii. *On being asked which one of the parents deserved better treatment, Prophet Muhammad (peace be upon him) mentioned mother and he repeated this thrice.*

29

Allah commands man to be kind to his parents. His mother carried him in pain and gave him birth in pain. The carrying of a child up to his weaning is a period of thirty months. When man reaches his full strength and is forty years old, he prays, 'O my Lord, enable me to thank You for Your favours which You did to me and my parents. Enable me to keep doing good which may please You. Make my children pious. I repent to You. I am a Muslim.'

(AL-AHQAF 46: 15)

The Qur'an recounts at length the hardship which a mother has to endure in carrying, giving birth to and feeding her child. It directs us to be kind to our parents and to pray for them but draws particular attention to the mother and all that she goes through for her children.

∾ 31 ∾

But he who tells his parents: 'What! Do you tell me that I will be raised alive (after death)? So many generations have passed before me and (they have not been raised alive).' His parents seek Allah's help and tell him: 'Woe to you! Have faith. Allah's promise is true.'

(AL-AHQAF 46: 17)

It is the parents' duty to instruct their children in the articles of Islamic faith, particularly belief in the One True God. This is a principle duty that both the mother and the father carry with regards to their children. It is a responsibility they both share and requires active participation, tact and leading by example on the part of both parents.

31

∽ 32 ∽

Your Lord has given the following commands:

- Do not worship anyone beside the One True God, Allah.
- Be kind to parents, whether one or both of them attain old age.
- Do not say to them any offensive word.
- Speak to them with respect.
- Be humble and kind to them.
- Keep praying: 'O my Lord, bestow Your mercy on them as they brought me up when I was small.'

(AL-ISRA' 17: 23-24)

This is yet another Qur'anic passage, urging us to be respectful and kind to our parents. This passage, containing a whole set of directives, instructs us to treat parents well and stresses that this applies to both mother and father whether both or only one of them is alive. It concludes with the reminder that we should pray for Allah's mercy on them both.

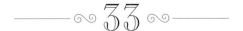

∾ 33 ∾

Allah has commanded man to be kind to his parents. However, if they (either of them) strive (to force) you to join with Me (in worship) anything of which you have no knowledge, then do not obey them. To Me is your return, and I shall let you know all that you have done.

(AL-'ANKABUT 29: 8)

※

The Qur'an makes it plain that despite one's tremendous love, kindness and respect for parents, there is no obedience to them in sin, particularly polytheism and disbelief. In Islam everyone is responsible and answerable for their own conduct. Following someone blindly out of respect will be no defence in Allah's court.

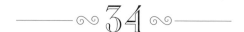

34

It is Allah Who created you from a single soul and out of it He made its spouse. This is so that man may find comfort in her. When he covers her, she grows heavy. Then they both pray to Allah, their Lord, saying: 'If You give us a healthy child, we will thank You.'

(AL-A'RAF 7: 189)

34

In Islam sexual relations between a husband and wife do not carry any hint of being dirty or shameful, rather for a couple to want to start a family and build a life together is the natural progression. The above Qur'anic passage portrays a perfectly united couple praying to and thanking Allah for His gifts.

It is permitted for you to approach your wives on the night of fasts. They are your garments and you their garments. Allah knows what you did secretly. He has turned to you in mercy and forgiven you. So now approach your wives. Seek what Allah has decided for you.

(AL-BAQARAH 2: 187)

✴

This passage clarifies that sexual union between a husband and wife during the day while fasting is not allowed. However, they may approach each other sexually after the fast is over.

The use of the metaphor of garments to describe the nature of the bond between husband and wife is very meaningful. It indicates their dependence upon each other: one remains incomplete without the other. Moreover, it expresses their mutual closeness, intimacy, comfort and respect.

∽ 36 ∽

Their Lord accepted their (women's) prayer, saying: 'I do not lay to waste the action of any of you, male or female. Each of you is from one another.'

(Al 'Imran 3: 195)

This Divine promise of equal reward for men and women was occasioned when some women conveyed to the Prophet Muhammad (peace be upon him) their uneasiness. They thought that the Qur'an addressed men alone, without mentioning women specifically. The above passage puts men and women on the same footing and assures women that they too will be rewarded for their good actions.

37

Those who annoy believing men and women, without justice, are guilty of a false charge and an open sin.

(AL-AHZAB 33:58)

※

The Qur'an condemns ill treatment towards the believers and makes a point of mentioning both men and women in this regard. Such teachings went a long way in raising the stature of women in 7ᵗʰ century Arabia where women did not have any right or social standing; they were considered subhuman.

～ 38 ～

(Lawful to you in marriage) are chaste women from among the believers and the people of the Book. This when you give them their dower and become their protector in marriage. This should not be for fornication and for taking them as secret lovers.

(AL-MA'IDA 5: 5)

In Islam marriage is a solemn, serious commitment: a man is asked to select a chaste believing woman, pay her dower and carry out his duties as a husband. Marriage is meant to guarantee women with financial, emotional and physical protection.

⸞ 39 ⸞

Marry women of your choice – two or three or four. If you fear that you cannot deal justly with them, then marry only one or a female captive of war. This is more likely to avoid injustice.

(AL-NISA' 4: 3)

✳

Marriage in Islam is a contract between two consenting adults. For a variety of reasons there is nonetheless a provision for polygamy. However, this provision is inextricably linked with justice. The Qur'an pointedly asks men not to be unjust to their wives, especially when they have more than one wife. Going as far as discouraging them by pointing out that if justice cannot be done then marry only one.

39

O Prophet, when believing women come
to you, ask them to pledge to you that
they will:
- not take any partner with Allah,
- not steal or have sex outside marriage,
- not kill children,
- not slander,
- not invent any falsehood, and
- not disobey you in anything good.

(AL-MUMTAHINAH 60: 12)

*This moral code covers both beliefs and actions on
the part of women in order to ensure a happy, peaceful society.*

O Prophet, ask the believing men to lower their gaze and to guard their private parts. That is better for them. Allah is aware of all that they do.

Ask the believing women to lower their gaze and to guard their private parts.

They should not display their beauty except what appears itself. They should draw their veils over their bosom. They should not display their charms, except before their husband, father, husband's father, sons, husband's sons, brothers, brother's sons, sister's sons, women, slave girls or those male servants who do not have any sexual interest and such children who are not aware of the private parts of women.

The believing women should not strike their feet in order to draw attention to their hidden ornaments.

O believers, all of you should repent to
Allah so that you may get success.

(AL-NUR 24: 31)

Significantly enough, the Qur'anic directive for lead-
ing a chaste life is addressed in an equal measure to
both men and women. The latter are advised further
not to make a show of their feminine charms. The
above detailed guidelines underline the importance
which Islam attaches to a pure, stable social order.

42

Men are the protectors and maintainers of
women. For Allah has given the one more
(strength) than the other, and because men
spend their wealth on supporting them.
So the pious women are obedient and
guard the rights of men in their absence
under Allah's protection.

As to those women on whose part you
fear disloyalty and ill-conduct, (first)

advise them, (next) refuse to share their bed, and (last) beat them (lightly). If they return to obedience, do not look for ways to harm them. Allah is Most Exalted, the Greatest.

(al-Nisa' 4: 34)

Since Islam does not lay any financial burden on women, it charges men with the responsibility to support their wife and family and hence his role as the protector. The Qur'an urges women to be faithful to their husband. It prescribes graded corrective measures for tackling those women who are guilty of serious moral wrongdoings. Hadiths clarify that beating, suggested as the last resort, should be nominal and not cause any injury. Wife-beating or any form of domestic violence is completely ruled out in Islam and is a serious offence in itself.

43

43

The believers keep praying: 'O our Lord, grant us such wives and children who will be a joy to our eyes. Make us a role model for the pious.'

(AL-FURQAN 25: 74)

The ideal Qur'anic wife and children are pious, engaged in doing good, and hence a source of joy. The benchmark of excellence that Allah places on a wife and children is their level of submission to Allah.

44

44

Allah sent Messengers before you
(O Prophet Muhammad). He gave them
wives and children.

(AL-RA'D 13: 38)

❋

*Islam, an action-orientated faith, does not recognise
any form of monasticism. The Qur'an affirms that
Messengers of God, the noblest souls, had wives and
families and they all participated in family life.*

45

∾ 45 ∾

O believers, there are enemies for you among your wives and children. Be careful about them. If you pardon, overlook and forgive, you should realise that Allah is Most Forgiving, Most Merciful.

(al-Taghabun 64: 14)

Whereas having a family is a Divine gift, it has the possibility of becoming a test and a trial hence the warning. Care needs to be taken that religious principles and responsibilities are not neglected in one's love and attempts to provide for them.

⟶ ∾ 46 ∾ ⟵

Those who torment the believing men
and women and do not repent, there is the
punishment of Hell for them: they will
have the penalty of burning [in Hellfire].

(al-Buruj 85: 10)

❊

*The Qur'an warns those who offend the believers, be
they men or women.*

47

Allah presents for the believers the example of the wife of Pharaoh. She prayed: 'O my Lord, build for me a house near You in Paradise. Deliver me from Pharaoh and his evil actions, and the wrongdoing people.'

Allah also presents the example of Mary, the daughter of Imran. She guarded her chastity. Allah breathed into her body of His spirit. She testified to the words of her Lord and His Books. She was one of the obedient (servants of Allah).

(AL-TAHRIM 66: 11-12)

Here the Qur'an cites two women as role models for all those who believe – the Pharaoh's believing and discerning wife; and the chaste Mary, mother of Prophet Jesus.

48

Mention also the woman (Mary) who guarded her chastity. Allah breathed into her of His spirit. He made her and her son (Prophet Jesus) a sign for all people.

(AL-ANBIYA' 21: 91)

The Qur'an projects Mary as a Divine sign for all people.

49

—— ⁓ 49 ⁓ ——

Allah inspired Moses's mother: 'Suckle your child. However, when you fear for his life, cast him into the river. Do not fear or grieve. We will restore him to you and appoint him one of Our Messengers.'

(al-Qasas 28: 7)

That Allah instructed Prophet Moses's mother and comforted and consoled her directly speaks volumes about her elevated status and the important status that Islam gives to mothers.

50

∞ 50 ∞

'I found there a woman (the Queen of Sheba) ruling over them and she has all things. She has a mighty throne.'

(AL-NAML 27: 22)

⁂

Prophet Solomon (peace be upon him) received the above report about the Queen of Sheba. She appears in the Qur'an as an intelligent, fair-minded and powerful woman.

∽ 51 ∽

Women have the same rights over men, as men have over them in accordance with what is fair. But men have a degree over them. Allah is Almighty, the Wisest.

(AL-BAQARAH 2: 228)

The Qur'an is clear in informing women of their rights as identical to those of men. However, it states that men have a degree over them and this has been explained in terms of the responsibility that a husband has of spending on his family out of his means.

52

O people, fear your Lord Who created all of you from a single being. And out of this He created man's mate. And out of these two He spread many men and women. Fear Allah in Whose name you demand your mutual rights and maintain the ties of kinship. Surely, Allah is ever watchful over you.

(AL-NISA' 4: 1)

53

The Qur'an points out that all men and women share the same line of descent. Furthermore, throughout, the Qur'an emphasises ties of kinship. It is worth adding that these ties originate with women and hence her pivotal role and status in the Divine scheme for the perpetuation of the human race.

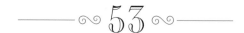

53

Give women their dower cheerfully (as a duty). However, if they willingly forego any part of it to you, you may take it happily.

(AL-NISA' 4: 4)

※

The Qur'an is very particular about protecting the financial interests of women, and hence the above directive with regards to the cheerful payment of dower to the wife as a duty. It also brings to light such a perfect understanding between a husband and wife where she may willingly forego all or part of what is her due, however, the choice is hers to make.

∼ 54 ∼

O believers, it is not lawful for you to inherit women against their will. Do not confine (the widow) that you may take away from them some of what you gave them, except when they are openly guilty of immoral conduct. Live with your wives with kindness. If you dislike them, it may be that Allah may have placed much good for you in something which you dislike.

(AL-NISA' 4: 19)

✳

In pre-Islamic Arab society, a widow was treated as a Commodity; she did not have rights of her own or an identity of her own. Islam restored her dignity and status as an individual. This ayah also indicates that she is free to choose her marriage partner and cannot be forced against her will. The passage also pointedly asks men to live in kindness with their wives and reminds them that oftentimes human beings fail to see the goodness in something that they think they dislike.

∞ 55 ∞

If you fear differences between the two
(man and wife), appoint two arbiters, one
from his, and one from her family. If both
want to set things right, Allah will bring
about peace between them. Allah is All
Knowing, All Aware.

(AL-NISA' 4: 35)

*The Qur'an commands that marital disputes should
be resolved by arbitration where both husband and
wife have equal representation and both arbiters
have an equal role and responsibility.*

﹏ 56 ﹏

You cannot treat your wives with (perfect) justice, even if you want to do so. Yet do not turn fully towards one, leaving the other neglected. If you reform and fear Allah, He is Most Forgiving, Most Merciful.

If the two separate, Allah will provide them out of His bounty. Allah is Limitless, the Wisest.

(al-Nisaʾ 4: 129–130)

57

This Qurʾanic call for justice and fairness in treating wives is worthy of note. Men are urged to fear Allah on this count. Furthermore, financial protection should not force a wife to put up with an unhappy marriage. Allah promises her financial help and support out of His boundless bounty.

—∞ **57** ∞—

Marry those among you who are single (men or women). Marry those of your male and female slaves who are pious. If they are poor, Allah will make them rich out of His grace. Allah is Boundless, All Knowing.

(al-Nur 24: 33)

＊

Islam encourages marriage irrespective of a person's financial situation Allah provides for everyone out of His grace.

∽ 58 ∽

O Prophet, Allah heard the statement of the woman who argued with you about her husband. She appealed to Allah. He heard what both of you said. Allah is All Hearing, All Seeing.

(al-Mujadilah 58: 1)

✳

This ayah reflects Allah's concern for a woman in distress and is in relation to Khawla bint Thalabah; she complained to the Prophet (peace be upon him) about her husband who had severed the marital tie by pronouncing zihar. This was a pre-Islamic form of separation whereby the husband declared his wife to be like the back of his mother hence did not have sexual relations with her but would not divorce her either hence leaving her in limbo. Like many other such discriminatory practices, Islam outlawed zihar.

59

∽ 59 ∾

Those among you who divorce their wives by *zihar* (declaring their wives to be their mothers) should realise that they are not their mothers. Their mothers are those who gave birth to them. Those guilty of *zihar* use dishonourable and false words. Yet God is Most Pardoning, Most Forgiving. Those guilty of *zihar*, if they want to take back what they said, they should free a slave before they touch each other (as husband and wife). You are ordered to do this. God is aware of your actions. If he cannot free a slave, he should fast for two months, without a break, before they touch each other.

(AL-MUJADILAH 58: 2-4)

60

The Qur'an prescribed a severe penalty for those guilty of zihar.

Divorce may be given twice, then there should be either honourable retaining or separation with kindness. It is not lawful for you to take back anything (while dissolving marriage) of what you have given to your wives, except when both the parties may not be able to follow the limits set by Allah. If you (judges) fear that they will not be able to follow the limits set by Allah, there is no blame upon either of them, if she gives something for her release from marriage. These are the limits set by Allah. So do not cross these. Those who cross the limits set by Allah, they are wrongdoers.

(AL-BAQARAH 2: 229)

61

Since marriage in Islam is a contract between two consenting adults, there is also a provision for either of them to opt out of it. Both husband and wife have the right to seek divorce but Allah makes a point of

directing that it should be conducted with honour and kindness. Additionally, the husband is specifically addressed to be kind and generous to his divorced wife. Let this, however, be added that in the sight of Allah divorce is a most regrettable and hateful act. For it sours relations not only between the couple but also among the near and dear ones of both the families. Furthermore, it plays havoc with the psyche and future of the children of the divorced couple. Nonetheless, for a variety of considerations, there exists the provision for divorce.

There is no blame upon them if they (the divorced husband and wife) re-unite, provided that they think they will be able to follow the limits set by God.

(AL-BAQARAH 2: 230)

The Qur'an emphasises that both partners in this contract are equal in making a decision; it is one of mutual consent, not duress.

When you divorce your wives and they
reach the end of their waiting period,
either retain them honourably or release
them honourably. But do not retain them
in order to hurt them or by way of cross-
ing the limits. He who does so wrongs
himself. Do not take God's commands
lightly. Bring to mind God's favours to
you. And remember that He sent down
to you the Book and wisdom for your
instruction. Fear God and keep in mind
that God knows everything.

(AL-BAQARAH 2:231)

*Qur'anic rulings on divorce are constantly inter-
spersed with warning and repeated advice to the
husband to be kind and generous to his divorced wife
notwithstanding their estranged relations. Throughout, the Qur'an seeks to instill piety and fear of God
in the husband.*

63

[During the waiting period] lodge the divorced women according to your income where you live. Do not hurt them in order to make life difficult for them. If they are pregnant, support them until the delivery. If they feed your child, give them their wage.

(AL-TALAQ 65:6)

∼ 64 ∼

When you divorce your wives, and they complete their waiting term, do not prevent them from marrying men, if they mutually agree in a customary way. This instruction is for all those who believe in Allah and the Last Day. This is the cleaner and purer way for you. Allah knows but you do not.

(AL-BAQARAH 2: 232)

*

According to the Qur'an, divorced women are at liberty to remarry. It warns those who obstruct this natural course.

65

65

O Believers, when you marry believing women and divorce them before touching them, you may not ask them to observe the waiting period. Give them some provision and release them in an honourable manner.

(AL-AHZAB 33: 49)

66

66

Mothers (divorced ones) may suckle their children for two years, if the father desires the completion of this period. It is obligatory on the father to bear the cost of their food and clothing in a fair manner. No one is burdened with more than they can bear.

No mother is to be treated unfairly on account of her child. No father is to be treated unfairly on account of his child… If both, father and mother, after mutual consultation, decide on weaning, there is no blame on them. Likewise, there is no blame upon them if they decide on a foster mother for their children.

(al-Baqarah 2:233)

∞ 67 ∞

The wives of men who die shall observe the waiting period of four months and ten days. When they reach the end of this term, there is no blame upon you if these women decide something about themselves in a fair manner. Allah is aware of all that you do.

(al-Baqarah 2: 234)

Like divorced women, widows are also free to remarry. Under the Islamic law they are not only able to remarry, they are encouraged to remarry and to play an active part in taking this decision.

68

There is no blame upon you if you hint at a marriage proposal to such women or keep it in your heart… But do not make a secret contract with them. Speak only in a fair manner. Do not resolve on marriage until the prescribed term is over. Keep in mind that God knows what is in your hearts.

(al-Baqarah 2: 235)

This Qur'anic directive is with regards to widows and directs men to behave sensitively towards women undergoing a highly emotional and traumatic experience. Their self-esteem and modesty are to be protected and they should not be exploited.

69

Do not marry the women whom your father married. What is past is past. It was indeed a shameful, loathsome and evil practice.

(al-Nisa' 4: 22)

Islam put an end to this pre-Islamic Arab practice. The use of as many as three strong adjectives, 'shameful, loathsome and evil' for condemning this practice illustrates the insistence in Islam on eradicating all forms of injustice to women.

⟿ 70 ⟾

Those who accuse chaste women, and do not produce four witnesses, flog them with eighty whips. And after this never accept their testimony. They are wicked.

(AL-NUR 24: 4)

✻

The Qur'an takes a very serious stance against slandering innocent women. The pre-requisite of having four first-hand eye witnesses serves as a deterrent against harassing and falsely implicating innocent women. Furthermore, the Qur'an prescribes a deterrent corporeal punishment for the guilty and their testimony is disqualified forever.

71

There is a curse in this life and the Next on those who slander chaste, innocent believing women. There is severe punishment for them. On the Day of Judgement their tongues, their hands and their feet will testify as to what they used to do. On that Day God will pay them back with justice. And they will realise that God is truth and that He makes the truth clear.

(AL-NUR 24: 23–25)

72

✳

In this Qur'anic passage a stern warning is made of severe punishment in the Hereafter for those who make false accusations of sexual misconduct against women.

~ *72* ~

O believers, do not enter houses other than your own unless you take permission and greet those inside them. This is best for you. It is expected you will follow this.

(AL-NUR 24: 27)

These Islamic norms are meant to prevent wrong by regulating day-to-day conduct and introducing a process of social reform that ensures the protection of privacy.

73

∞ *73* ∞

It is not fitting for a believer, man or woman, when a matter has been decided by Allah and His Messenger, to have any option about their decision. If anyone disobeys Allah and His Messenger, he/she is indeed on a clearly wrong Path.

(AL-AHZAB 33: 36)

❋

Allah expects men and women to demonstrate the same level of obedience in following the principles set by Allah and His Messenger. They will be rewarded and punished to the same degree for their actions, for they are equal in the sight of Allah.

~ 74 ~

Those who accuse their wives and have no witness except themselves, their testimony is: he should testify four times swearing by God that he is speaking the truth. He should say on the fifth time that God's curse be on him if he is lying. The woman will, however, not be punished if she testifies four times swearing by God that he is lying. She should say on the fifth time that God's curse be on her, if he is speaking the truth (by way of his accusation).

(AL-NUR 24: 6–9)

75

In the case of lian (husband's charge of infidelity against his wife) the words of both the husband and wife carry equal weight. If both persist in their stance, after taking oath four times in God's name, their marriage is annulled.

—— ∽ *75* ∾ ——

If you decide on taking a wife in place of another, do not take back anything from her, even if you had given her a heap of gold. Will you take it back by slandering her and doing an outrageous wrong? How can you take back after you have enjoyed each other and after they took a solemn pledge from you?

(AL-NISA' 4:20–21)

76

The Qur'an speaks of the sexual enjoyment of both husband and wife. In Islam, a woman is not a sex object, to be used and then dumped. A husband and wife are equal partners, marriage is a solemn pledge and both share the joys of sex within marriage.

76

God reminds you of the verses in this Book about the orphan women. Yet you do not give them the shares prescribed for them, and yet you still want to marry them (out of greed).

(AL-NISA' 4:127)

Orphaned women were doubly marginalised in society and hence received greater attention in the Qur'an. Men are exhorted to be very particular about the rights of women and especially orphan women.

77

Umm Salmah reported the Prophet ﷺ as having said: 'A woman who dies while her husband is pleased with her, will go straight to Paradise.'

(TIRMIDHI, 'K. AL-RIDA' HADITH NO. 1141)

— ∽ 78 ∽ —

The Prophet  remarked: 'A man is in charge of his house. A wife is the custodian of her husband's house and her children. Each one of you is accountable for what is under your care. Allah will hold you to account for the same.'

(BUKHARI, 'K. AL-AHKAM')

— ∽ 79 ∽ —

Many women visited the Prophet  and complained to him against their husbands of ill treatment. Upon this he declared: 'Those among you who do not treat their wives well are not good people.'

(ABU DAWUD, 'K. AL-NIKAH')

∞ 80 ∞

The Prophet ﷺ announced: 'One who does not bury his daughter alive, does not look down upon her and does not prefer his son to her, will be granted Paradise by Allah.'

(Abu Dawud, 'K. al-Adab')

∞ 81 ∞

The Prophet ﷺ stated: 'One usually marries a woman for these considerations: her wealth, her noble lineage, her beauty and her religious mind. You should marry one who is religiously minded.'

(Muslim, 'K. al-Rida')

~ 82 ~

The Prophet  warned: 'Allah has forbidden you the following: displeasing your mother and burying your daughter alive.'

(Bukhari, 'K. al-Adab' Hadith no. 5975)

~ 83 ~

The Prophet  stated: 'As I passed by Paradise, I heard someone reciting the Qur'an there. On my enquiry, angels told me that Harithah ibn Numan was reciting the Qur'an.' He added: 'This was his reward for doing good to parents. Harithah had been extremely kind to his mother.'

(Mishkat, 'K. al-Adab' Hadith no. 4926)

~ 84 ~

Ibn Umar reported that someone called on the Prophet ﷺ and informed him of having committed a major sin. He then asked: 'O Messenger of Allah, what is my atonement?' To this he responded: 'Is your mother alive?' When he replied in the negative, he directed him to take good care of his maternal aunt (which may atone his sin).

(Trimidhi, 'K. al-Birr wa al-Sila' Hadith no. 1904)

~ 85 ~

The Prophet ﷺ remarked: 'Of all the bounties in this world, a pious wife is the best.'

(Ibn Majah, 'K. al-Nikah')

~ 86 ~

The Prophet ﷺ advised: 'Allah has forbidden for you any disobedience and injustice to your mother.'

(Bukhari, 'K. al-Adab')

~ 87 ~

The Prophet ﷺ declared: 'Allah has allowed you (O women) to go out for meeting your needs.'

(Bukhari, 'K. Kharaj al-Nisa')

88

The Prophet ﷺ warned: 'One who looks lustfully at a woman will have molten lead poured into his eyes on the Day of Judgement.'

(Al-Hidaya, 'K. al-Karahiya')

89

The Prophet ﷺ is on record having declared: 'A woman who offers the five obligatory prayers, fasts during the month of Ramadan, protects her chastity and obeys her husband is most likely to be rewarded with Paradise.'

(Sahih Ibn Hibban, Hadith no. 4163)

∞ 90 ∞

Umm Hisham bint Harithah ibn al-Numan, a lady Companion, said: 'I learned *Qaf. Wal-Qur'an al-Majid* (Surah 50 of the Qur'an) from the Prophet ﷺ. He used to recite it from the *minbar* (pulpit) every Friday when he addressed the congregation.'

(Sahih Muslim, 6/162, 'K. al-Jumu'ah')

84

∞ 91 ∞

Fatimah bint Qays related: 'People were called to prayer, so I rushed with the others to the mosque, and prayed behind the Messenger of Allah. I used to stand in the first row of women, which was behind the last row of men.'

(Muslim, 18/84, 'Kitab al-Fitan')

— ༺ 92 ༻ —

Umm Atiyah reported: 'The Messenger of Allah asked us (women) to bring to the Eid prayers all women, including girls and he directed that those who were menstruating should keep away from the prayer spot.'

<small>(Muslim, 6/178, 179, 'K. Salat al-Idayn')</small>

— ༺ 93 ༻ —

Umm Salmah recounted: 'I used to hear the people talking about *al-hawd* (the cistern at the grand assembly on the Day of Judgement), though I had never heard about it from the Messenger of Allah. One day, whilst a young girl was combing my hair, I heard the Messenger of Allah saying, "O people!" I told the young girl, "Leave me alone now." She said: "That call is for men only; he is not calling women."

I said, "I am one of the people (and he is addressing people)." The Messenger of Allah said: "I am the one who will be at the cistern before you. So be careful, lest one of you should come to me and be driven away like a stray camel. I will ask the reason and I will be told: 'You do not know what innovations they wrought after your death,' and I will say, 'Away with them!'"

According to another report also narrated by Muslim, the Prophet (peace be upon him) said: 'I will say, "Away, away with the one who changed (the religion) after my death!"'

(MUSLIM, 15/56, 54, 'K. AL-FADAIL')

Khawlah bint Thalabah reported to the Prophet ﷺ about *zihar* committed by her husband. In the light of the Qur'anic command about *zihar*, recorded in verses 1-4 of Surah al-Mujadilah, he told her: 'As expiation your husband should set a slave free.' When she told him that he did not have the means to do so, he directed that he should fast consecutively for two months. She submitted: 'He is an old man. He cannot fast.' Then he said: 'Let him feed dates to sixty people.' She submitted: 'He does not have that amount of dates either. I will nonetheless give him some.' The Prophet ﷺ told her: 'You have done something good. I too, will give some dates. Give these dates in charity.'

(IBN KATHIR, 'TAFSIR SURAH AL-MUJADILAH')

—∾ 95 ∾—

Caliph Umar ibn al-Khattab met Khawlah
outside a mosque and greeted her. She
said, 'O Umar, I have known you since
you were called the little Umar in Ukkaz
market. You used to carry a stick in your
hand in order to take care of your flock
of sheep. Fear Allah as you are Caliph.
Look after well those who are under your
care. One who fears punishment in the
Hereafter knows well that the Day is not
far away. Do not miss any opportunity for
doing good in this world.' Al-Jarud who
was present there said: 'O woman, you
have spoken too harshly to the Caliph.'
Umar, however interrupted him, saying:
'Let her speak. Do you not know she is
Khawlah? Allah on the high listened to
her plea. By Allah, I must listen to her.'

(Fath al-Bari, 8, 489. 'K. al-Tafsir')

96

Aishah said: 'May Allah have mercy on the Muhajir women. As soon as Allah ordered: *They should draw their wrapping garment over their bosoms* (AL-AHZAB 33: 59) they instantly covered their heads and faces.'

(FATH AL-BARI, 8, 489. 'K. AL-TAFSIR')

◦ 97 ◦

Muslim women were present also at the Treaty of ʿAqabah, which took place in secret, under the cover of darkness. This treaty played an important role in supporting the Prophet ﷺ. Among the delegation of Ansar were two women of status and virtue: Nasibah bint Kaʿb al-Maziniyah, and Umm Mani ʿAsma bint ʿAmr al-Sulamiyah, the mother of Muʿadh ibn Jabal.

An old Muslim woman, Ruqayqah bint Sayfi, was the first to alert the Prophet ﷺ about the Makkans' plot to assassinate him. He embarked upon his *hijrah* (migration to Madinah), leaving the land that was the most beloved to him on earth.

(Tabaqat ibn Saʿd, 7/35)

Thalabah ibn Abi Malik reported: 'Umar ibn al-Khattab distributed some clothes among the women of Madinah. There was one good piece left. Someone suggested: "Give this to the grand-daughter of the Messenger of Allah, i.e. Umm Kulthum bint 'Ali." However, 'Umar said: "Umm Salit is more entitled to it." Umm Salit was one of the Ansar women who had pledged their allegiance to the Prophet ﷺ. 'Umar added: "She carried a water-skin for us on the day of the battle of Uhud."'

(Fath al-Bari, 6/7420.'K. al-Jihad')

A Companion sought Prophet Muhammad's advice. 'O Messenger of Allah, who among people is most deserving of my good treatment?' He said: 'Your mother.' The man asked: 'Then who?' He replied: 'Your mother.' The man again asked: 'Then who?' He repeated: 'Your mother.' The man persisted: 'Then who?' It was then that he said: 'Your father.'

(Sharh as-Sunnah, 13/4. 'K. al-Istidhan')

∽ 100 ∾

One example of the strength and maturity of Muslim women's character, and the freedom that they enjoyed in early Islam to express their opinions, is the criticism voiced by a woman who was listening to the Caliph 'Umar ibn al-Khattab. He forbade huge dower and insisted that dower should be limited to a reasonable amount. It was then that this woman stood up and said: 'You have no right to do that, O Umar!' He asked: 'Why not?' She replied: 'Because Allah says:

93

But if you decide to take one wife in place of another, even if you had given the latter a whole treasure for dower, take not the least bit of it back. Would you take it by slander and a manifest wrong?'

(al-Nisa' 4: 20)

Umar exclaimed: 'The woman is right, and I stand corrected.'

(Fath al-Bari, 'K. al-Nikah')

∼101∼

Some Ansar women requested the Prophet ﷺ: 'Fix a day for us when we may learn something valuable from you, for men take all your time and leave nothing for us.' He told them: 'Your appointment is at the house of so-and-so (one of the women).' So, he visited them there and imparted the teachings of Islam.

(Fatḥ al-Bārī, 1/195, 'K. al-'Ilm')

∼102∼

Al-Zuhri said: 'If the knowledge of Aishah were to be gathered and compared to the knowledge of all the other wives of the Prophet ﷺ and of all other women, her knowledge would be greater.'

(Al-Istiab, 4/1883)

∾103∾

Someone asked the Prophet: 'Which deed is liked most by Allah?' He said, 'Prayer offered on time.' He then asked: 'Then what?' He replied: 'Kindness and respect towards parents.'

(SHARH AL-SUNNAH, 176, 'K. AL-SALAT')

∾104∾

Asma bint Abu Bakr recounted: 'My mother came to me, and she was an unbeliever at that time. I asked the Prophet ﷺ: "My mother has come to me and needs my help. Should I help her?" He replied: "Yes, keep in touch with her and help her."'

(SHARH AL-SUNNAH, 13/13, 'K. AL-BIRR')

105

The Prophet  remarked: 'This world is for temporary stay and the best comfort in this world is a pious woman.'

(MUSLIM, 10/56, 'K. AL-RIDA')

106

Al-Khansa bint Khidam reported: 'My father got me married to his nephew, and I did not like this match. So I complained to the Messenger of Allah. He told me: "Accept what your father has arranged." I said: "I do not wish to accept what my father has arranged." He said: "Then this marriage is invalid, go and marry whoever you wish." I replied: "I accept what my father has arranged, but I wanted women to know that fathers have no right to force a marriage of their choice on their daughters."'

(FATH AL-BARI, 9/194. 'K. AN-NIKAH', AND IBN MAJAH, 1/602, 'K. AN-NIKAH')

∼∽107∾∼

Barirah was an Ethiopian slave girl of Utbah. He got her married to a slave, Mughith. At a later date Aishah bought Barirah and set her free. As a free woman she exercised her right and secured separation from her husband whom she did not like. This devastated Mughith and obsessed with love for his divorced wife, he followed her wherever she went, and cried publicly. While taking pity on him, the Prophet ﷺ asked Barirah: 'Why do you not go back to him?' She replied: 'O Messenger of Allah! Is this your command for me?' However, he replied that he meant only to recommend Mughith's case in view of his plight. Upon this she curtly told him: 'I am not at all interested in Mughith.'

(FATH AL-BARI, 9/408, 'K. AL-TALAQ')

97

⟿ 108 ⟿

Umm Sulaym's young son died while her husband was away. When he returned, she served him dinner. After they retired to bed, he made love to her. When he was about to sleep, she asked him: 'O Abu Talhah, what do you say, if someone takes back what he had lent to us?' He replied: 'It is perfectly fine.' It was then that she told him: 'Reconcile to the death of our son.' He grew furious, asking her as to why she let him have food and sex, without telling him first about the loss of their son. He reported the matter to the Prophet  who consoled him, saying: 'May Allah bless both of you.' After some time, she conceived and had a baby boy whom the Prophet ﷺ named Abdullah.

(MUSLIM, 16/11, 'K. FADAIL AL-SAHABAH')

109

Upon listening to the Qur'anic verse (al-Baqarah 2:245) 'Who among you will loan to Allah a good loan which he will return after multiplying it?', Abu Dardah gave in Allah's cause his big orchard consisting of four hundred trees. When he told his wife about it, she cheerfully said: 'You have struck a good bargain. This is a successful deal, O Abu Dardah.' Upon this the Prophet ﷺ exclaimed: 'Many date trees have lowered down their clusters, full of pearls and gems in Paradise for Abu Dardah.'

(Tafsir Ibn Kathir, Surah al-Baqarah 2: 245)

Abu Hurayrah reported the Prophet as having said: 'May Allah have mercy on that husband who gets up at night and wakes up his wife to pray. And if she does not get up, he sprinkles water on her face. May Allah have mercy on that wife who gets up at night to pray and wakes up her husband to pray. And if he does not get up, she sprinkles water on his face.'

(ABU DAWUD, 2/45, 'K. AL-SALAH')

111

Aishah recounted: 'Whenever Fatimah came into the room, the Prophet ﷺ would stand up, welcome her, kiss her on her forehead and offer her his seat. And whenever the Prophet ﷺ entered the room, she would stand up, take his hand, welcome him, kiss him on his forehead and offer him her seat. When she came to see him during his terminal illness, he as usual, welcomed her and kissed her.'

(FATH AL-BARI, 8/135, 'K. AL-MAGHAZI')

101

Abu Hurayrah recounted that the Prophet ﷺ said: 'Whoever has three daughters and brings them up and shares their joys and sorrow, Allah will admit him/her to Paradise on account of their love and affection for their daughters.' A companion present there asked: 'O Messenger of Allah, what if one has only two daughters?' He replied: 'The same, even if he/she has only two daughters.' Another Companion asked: 'What if one has only one daughter?' To this he replied: 'The same, even if he/she has only one daughter.'

(AL-HAKIM, 4/176, 'K. AL-BIRR')

 113

According to the Tabarani, the Prophet ﷺ said: 'A member of my community who brings up and supports three daughters or three sisters until they come of age will accompany me in Paradise like this.' While saying this he joined his middle finger with his index finger.

(Tabarani, al-Mujam al-Awsat, Hadith no. 5578)

 114

The Prophet ﷺ advised: 'O Muslim women, do not think that any gift is too small to give to a neighbour, even if it be only a sheep's foot.'

(Sharh as-Sunnah, 6/141, 'K. al-Zakat')

It is reported that a Companion said:
'O Messenger of Allah, such-and-such
woman spends her nights in prayer, fasts
during the day, and she gives in charity, but
she offends her neighbours with her sharp
tongue.' The Prophet ﷺ said: 'Her good
deeds will be of no avail: she is among the
people of Hell.' Another Companion said,
'And so-and-so offers only the obligatory
prayers, gives charity in the form of only
the left-over food, but does not offend
anyone.' The Prophet ﷺ remarked: 'She is
among the people of Paradise.'

(Bukhari, al-Adab al-Mufrad, 1/210)

— ∾ 116 ∾ —

Once Aishah made a derogatory reference
to Safiyah's short stature. Upon hearing
this, the Prophet ﷺ said: 'You have spoken
a word that, if it were to be mixed with
the sea, it would pollute the whole sea.'

(ABU DAWUD, 4/371, 'K. AL-ADAB' AND
TIRMIDHI, 4/660, 'K. SIFAT AL-QIYAMAH')

— ∾ 117 ∾ —

Jahimah called on the Prophet ﷺ and said:
'O Messenger of Allah! I intend to join
the battle and have come to seek your
permission.' He enquired: 'Is your mother
alive?' 'Yes,' replied he. The Prophet ﷺ
told him: 'Then attend to her because
Paradise lies at her feet.'

(SUNAN AL-NASAI, 'K. AL-JIHAD', HADITH NO. 3104)

∾ 118 ∾

Abu Tufail reported: 'I saw the Messenger of Allah distributing meat at Jarana when a woman approached him. He spread out his sheet for her and she took her seat. I enquired: "Who is she"? I was told: "She is his foster mother."'

(ABU DAWUD, 'K. AL-ADAB', HADITH NO. 5144)

∾ 119 ∾

Muawiyah asked: 'O Messenger of Allah! What right does one owe to his wife?' He replied: 'You should give her the same food which you take and give her clothes when you have clothes. Do not slap or revile her.'

(IBN MAJAH, 'ABWAB AL-NIKAH' P. X, 327)

∽ 120 ∽

Abu Hurayrah reported that the Messenger of Allah said: 'The best believer is he who is of perfect conduct, and the best of you are those who are kind to their wives.'

(Tirmidhi, 'Abwab al-Manaqib' 1, 138)

∽ 121 ∽

Abu Hurayrah reported that the Messenger of Allah said: 'A previously married woman cannot be re-married till she gives her consent. Likewise, an unmarried girl cannot be married without obtaining her consent.' On being asked how she should give her consent, he clarified that her silence may also be taken as her consent.

(Ibn Taiymiyyah, Majmua al-Fatawa, 32, 39-40)

⁓ 122 ⁓

According to Abu Hurayrah, the Prophet ﷺ said: 'A girl's consent should be taken about her marriage. If she remains silent about a proposal, it may be taken as her consent. However, if she refuses, she should not be subjected to any compulsion.'

(BUKHARI, 'K. AL-NIKAH' HADITH NO. 4766)

⁓ 123 ⁓

Ibn Umar reported that the Messenger of Allah said: 'The most detestable of lawful things in the sight of Allah is divorce.'

(ABU DAWUD, 'K. AL-TALAQ')

124

Muadh ibn Jabal recounted that the Prophet  said: 'There is nothing better in the sight of Allah than freeing a slave. There is nothing worse in the sight of Allah than divorce.'

(Abu Dawud, 'K. al-Talaq')

125

Jabir ibn Abdullah reported that the Messenger of Allah said: 'Fear Allah regarding women. You have married them with the pledge in the name of Allah and made their body lawful for you in the name of Allah. They have rights regarding their food and clothing according to your means.'

(Muslim, 'K. al-Hajj')

126

Anas reported that the Messenger of Allah said: 'Seeking knowledge is compulsory for every Muslim male and Muslim female.'

(Ibn Majah, 'Muqadimah')

127

Wail ibn Hujr reported that a woman in the Prophet's day went to the mosque to offer prayer. A man raped her on the way. She raised the alarm but he ran away. She reported the matter to passers-by. They got hold of him and presented him before the Messenger of Allah. He said to her: 'Go back home. Allah has forgiven you.' However, he said about the rapist: 'Stone him to death.'

(Tirmidhi, Jamey, 'Abwab al-Hudud' Hadith no. 1454)

— ∾ 128 ∾ —

Aishah reported: 'I asked: O Messenger of Allah, Is there *Jihad* for women?' He replied: 'Yes, there is *Jihad* for them in which there is no fighting i.e. performing *Hajj* and *Umrah*.'

(IBN MAJAH, 'K. AL-JIHAD' HADITH NO. 2901)

— ∾ 129 ∾ —

Ibn Umar reported that the Messenger of Allah said: 'When your wife seeks permission to go to the mosque, you should not stop her.'

(MUSNAD AHMAD, HADITH NO. 5448)

Thawban narrated that Allah's Messenger said, 'A woman who seeks divorce from her husband without a valid reason, the fragrance of Paradise is forbidden for her.'

(TIRMIDHI, 'K. AL-TALAQ' HADITH NO. 1187)

131

Hind, Abu Sufyan's wife, said, 'O Allah's Messenger, Abu Sufyan is a miser. Is it wrong if I take from his belongings something to meet my and my children's needs?' He replied: 'Take according to your needs in a reasonable manner.'

(ABU DAWUD, SUNAN, 'K. AL-IJARA' HADITH NO. 3532)

～ 132 ～

Aishah narrated: 'The Prophet ﷺ said: "O Allah, I declare inviolable the rights of the two weak ones: orphans and women."'

(Ibn Majah, Sunan, 'K. al-Adab' Hadith no. 3678)

～ 133 ～

Aishah reported: 'A woman came to me with her two daughters. She asked me for food but she found nothing with me except one date-fruit, which I gave her. She divided it between her two daughters and took nothing. She then went away. When the Messenger of Allah came home, I narrated this to him. He said: "One who brings up daughters and is kind to them, will be protected against the Hellfire."'

(Muslim, 'K. al-Birr wa al-Sila' Hadith no. 2630)

—∞ 134 ∞—

Aishah reported that the Messenger of Allah never raised his hand against anyone, neither a servant nor a woman. However, he did fight bravely in the cause of Allah.

(Muslim, 'K. al-Fadail' Hadith no. 2328)

—∞ 135 ∞—

The Prophet ﷺ said: 'The believers with perfect faith are those who have the best morals, and the best of you are those who are very kind to your wives.'

(Tirmidhi, 'Abawab al-Rada', 1/ 138)

—∼ 136 ∼—

Both Aishah and Asma were party to the secret plan of the Prophet ﷺ and Abu Bakr regarding their migration from Makkah and Madinah.

(Bukhari, 'K. al-Buyu')

—∼ 137 ∼—

Rufaidah used to nurse Muslim soldiers wounded in Jihad. At the battle of Ahzab she pitched a tent near the trench in order to treat the injured Muslim soldiers.

(Bukhari, 'K. al-Maghazi' Hadith no. 4122)

❧ 138 ❧

Anas reported: 'I saw both Aishah and Umm Sulaim rushing to provide water to the wounded in the battle. They used to quickly refill their water skins and pour water into the mouths of those who could not drink on their own.'

(BUKHARI, 'K. MANAQIB AL-ANSAR' HADITH NO. 3811)

❧ 139 ❧

Rabi bint Maudh stated: 'We used to participate in battles along with the Prophet ﷺ. We would offer water to the wounded and took care of them. We also transported the injured to Madinah.'

(BUKHARI, 'K. AL-TAYYAB' HADITH NO. 5679)

— ❧ 140 ❧ —

Umm Mundhir bin Qays played an active role in the siege laid against Banu Quraizah, a Jewish tribe that was hostile to Muslims in Madinah.

(Bukhari, 'K. al-Maghazi' Hadith no. 4121)

— ❧ 141 ❧ —

The Prophet ﷺ remarked about his wife, Khadijah: 'Allah did not grant me her replacement who outdid her in excellence. She believed in me when everyone rejected me. She stood for me when everyone was bent on discrediting me. She helped me with her wealth when people had reduced me to a pauper.'

(Musnad Ahmad, Hadith no. 24745)

∽ 142 ∽

Saruq was asked whether Aishah was adept at the law of inheritance. To this he replied: 'By Allah I saw many Companions seeking her expert opinion on issues related to the law of inheritance.'

(HAKIM, MUSTADRAK, 4, 11)

∽ 143 ∽

After concluding the Hudaibiyah treaty the Prophet ﷺ directed the Companions to carry out the sacrifice of their animals, to be followed by the cutting of their own hair. He said this thrice yet none of them acted on his directive. They found it hard to reconcile to this treaty which they considered to be unfavourable to the Muslims. The Prophet ﷺ went to Umm Salmah and told her about their conduct. She submitted: 'O Messenger of Allah, if you want them to obey your command, you should go out, sacrifice your camel, shave your head, without saying a word to anyone.' As he did so, all the Companions rushed to carry out their sacrifice and cut their hair.

(BUKHARI, HADITH NO. 2732)

Aishah paid her tribute to Umm Salmah thus: 'I did not see any woman excelling her in matters of faith, piety, truthfulness, maintaining the ties of kinship and giving generously in charity.'

(AL-ISTIAB, 4, 316)

119

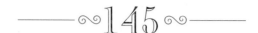

∾ 145 ∾

The lady Companions were very particular about *itikaf* (devotional retreat in the last ten days of Ramadan). When Aishah learnt about the Prophet's plan to perform *itikaf,* she and the other wives of the Prophet (peace be upon him) got their tents pitched.

(Abu Dawud, 'K. al-Siyam')

∾ 146 ∾

Umm Shurayk was a wealthy, generous lady. Her house served as a guest house for the Prophet's outstation guests.

(Nasai, 'K. al-Nikah')

— ❧ 147 ❧ —

The lady Companions regarded it as their duty to bring up orphans. Zaynab, the Prophet's wife, supported many orphans.

(BUKHARI, 'K. AL-ZAKAH')

— ❧ 148 ❧ —

The lady Companions took good care of the property and belongings of the orphans under their care. Aishah used to invest their money in trade.

(MALIK, MUWATTA, 'K. AL-ZAKAH')

— ∾ 149 ∾ —

Abu Talha sent his marriage proposal to Umm Sulaim. However, she turned it down because at that point he had not accepted Islam. She suggested his acceptance of Islam as dower. He obliged her and embraced Islam.

(Malik, Muwatta, 'K. al-Nikah')

— ∾ 150 ∾ —

Qaylah introduced herself as a business woman to the Prophet ﷺ and sought his rulings on several issues related to business and trade.

(Ibn Saad, Tabaqat, 8, 228)

∽ 151 ∾

Khansa joined the battle of Qadsiyah along with her four sons. All of her sons attained martyrdom in the battle.

(Ibn al-Athir, Usad al-Ghaba, 'K. al-Nisa', no. 6883)

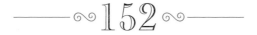

∽ 152 ∾

Zuhri stated: 'It has been the consistent practice to accept a single woman's testimony regarding issues which are special to them.'

(Ibn Hazm, al-Mahalla, 9, 395)

∾ 153 ∾

As many as 2210 Hadith reports are narrated on Aishah's authority.

(Sayr al-Sahabiat, 29)

∾ 154 ∾

Abu Musa Ashari said: 'Whenever we faced a difficult issue, Aishah always solved it by dint of her vast knowledge and insight.'

(Muslim, 'K. al-Ilm' Hadith no. 7555)

— ∞ 155 ∞ —

According to Urwah ibn Zubayr, Aishah surpassed everyone in her knowledge of the Qur'an, laws of inheritance, the lawful and the unlawful, jurisprudence, poetry, medicine, Arab history and genealogy.

(IBN SAAD, TABAQAT, VOL. 2)

— ∞ 156 ∞ —

Aishah was very generous. Abdullah ibn Zubayr reported that once Caliph Muawiyah sent her one hundred thousand dirhams. She gave them all in charity by evening. She was fasting that day, her slave girl informed her that there was nothing to break the fast with. It was then that she told her: 'You should have informed me of this earlier.'

(HAKIM, MUSTADRAK, 4, 113)

After the Qur'anic verse about *hijab* (segregation of sexes) had been revealed, Abdullah ibn Maktum, a blind Companion visited the Prophet's room in which his wives, Umm Salmah and Maimuna were present. He asked them to move away. Upon this they pointed out that Abdullah was a blind person. However, the Prophet ﷺ reminded them: 'But you are not blind. You can see him.'

(MUSNAD AHMAD, 6, 296)

126

The Prophet loved his daughter Fatimah dearly. Once he remarked: 'Fatimah is part of me. Whoever displeases her, hurts me.' Ali did not take another wife as long as Fatimah was alive.

(BUKHARI, I, 532)

— ∾ 159 ∾ —

While the Prophet ﷺ was praying in
Makkah, an unbeliever, Uqabah ibn Muit
placed a camel's entrails on his neck.
Although at that time Fatimah was a
small girl, only five years old, she rushed
to the scene, removed the rubbish and
condemned Uqabah for this misconduct.

(BUKHARI, I, 38)

— ∾ 160 ∾ —

Umamah was the daughter of the Prophet's daughter, Zaynab. She followed the
Prophet ﷺ everywhere. Once he entered
the mosque, carrying her on his shoulders.
More importantly, he led the prayer while
she was perched on his shoulders. When
he performed *ruku* and *sujud*, he placed
her on the floor and as he stood up, he put
her on his shoulders again. This is how he
offered his prayer.

(BUKHARI I, 74)

∽ 161 ∽

When King Negus sent the Prophet ﷺ an expensive necklace, he said that he would give it to his favourite family member. His wives presumed that Aishah will be his choice. However, he put it on his granddaughter Umamah's neck.

(IBN SAAD, TABAQAT, 8, 27)

∽ 162 ∽

Summaiyah holds the distinction of being the first Muslim martyr in the cause of Islam. Abu Jahl stabbed her to death in Makkah. When Abu Jahl was killed in the battle of Badr, the Prophet ﷺ told Yasir, Summaiyah's son: 'Look, Allah has decided the fate of your mother's killer.'

(AL-ISTIAB, 2, 760)

—∾ 163 ∾—

Umm Afiah accompanied the Prophet  in seven battles. She used to look after the injured, cook food, and provide first aid to the wounded.

(MUSLIM, 2, 105)

—∾ 164 ∾—

Umm Warqah was well versed in the Qur'an so the Prophet entrusted her with the assignment of leading prayer for women. At her request, he appointed a *muezzin* who used to make the call for prayer and she led the women's congregation.

(AL-ISABAH 1, 289)

— ∽ 165 ∾ —

Umm Hakim participated in the battle at Yarmuk. Her husband, Ikrimah was martyred in the same battle. As the battle raged, she appeared on the battle ground, carrying a heavy stick. She managed to kill seven enemy soldiers.

(AL-ISTIAB, 4, 425)

— ∽ 166 ∾ —

During her stay in Abysinnia, Asma bint Amis had noted the Christian practice of using a coffin for burial. She suggested the same to the Prophet ﷺ for Muslims, which was accepted with some modifications. Since then it has been the standard funerary practice among Muslims.

(IBN SAAD, TABAQAT, 8, 167)

— ∾ 167 ∾ —

On Eid day the Prophet ﷺ addressed a separate assembly of women. He urged them to donate in charity. Bilal, the Prophet's Companion, collected their generous donations, including their jewellery.

(Bukhari, 'K. al-Idayan')

— ∾ 168 ∾ —

As Uthman ibn Mazun almost renounced life, his wife neglected her upkeep. On enquiry she told Aishah that her husband fasts throughout the day and prays throughout the night. Hence she did not feel any need for maintaining herself. When Aishah recounted all this to the Prophet ﷺ, he summoned Uthman and asked him: 'Is my way not worth following? Look, I fear Allah and fast yet I break fast as well. I do pray yet I sleep. I marry women as well. Whoever deviates from my way is not one of us.'

(Bukhari, 'K. al-Nikah')

—∾ 169 ∾—

Umar is on record having admitted: 'By Allah, in the *Jahiliyyah* (pre-Islamic) period we used to look down upon women. However, Allah sent down to us commands about women's rights and share.'

(BUKHARI, 'K. AL-NIKAH', 2, 781)

—∾ 170 ∾—

132

Anas ibn Malik reported: 'Whenever the Prophet ﷺ marched out to battle, Umm Sulaim and some Ansar women used to accompany him. These women provided water and medical aid to the injured. They ensured a regular supply of water for soldiers.'

(BUKHARI, 'K. AL-MAGHAZI')

～171～

Aishah recounted: 'We, women wrapped in sheets used to accompany the Prophet ﷺ for Fajr prayer. Nobody could recognise us when we returned, for it was still dark then.'

(MUSLIM, 'K. AL-SALAH' HADITH NO. 647)

～172～

Zaynab bint Hajash was a skilled crafts-woman. She sold her craft work and gave her earnings in charity.

(USAD AL-GHABA, 5, 494)

133

 173

Zaynab bint Thaqafi, wife of Abdullah ibn Masud, was an accomplished crafts-woman. She used her earnings to support her husband. Since Abdullah was indigent, she bore all of his expenses.

(Usad al-Ghaba, 5, 263)

 174

An Ansar woman, who was a carpenter presented a pulpit to the Prophet ﷺ. He used to deliver his Friday prayer sermon from that pulpit.

(Bukhari, 'K. al-Buyu' Hadith no. 294)

—∾175∾—

Aishah said: 'I did not find anyone excelling Zaynab, the Prophet's wife in piety, truthfulness, generosity and maintaining the ties of kinship. She gained proximity with Allah through her charity.'

(Bukhari, 'K. al-Sadaqa' Hadith no. 7092)

—∾176∾—

Abdullah's wife, Zaynab reported: 'While I was in the mosque, I heard the Prophet ﷺ exhorting: "O women, give in charity, including even your jewellery."'

(Bukhari, 'K. al-Sadaqa' Hadith no. 7102)

—∞ 177 ∞—

Zaynab, Abdullah's wife reported that the Prophet ﷺ advised that women visiting the mosque should not wear perfume.

(MUSLIM, 'K. AL-MASJID' HADITH NO. 446)

—∞ 178 ∞—

Asma, Abu Bakr's daughter related: 'When Zubayr married me, he did not have any money or a servant. I used to look after his camel and horse. I did domestic chores as well. I also used to clean the plot of land, at some distance from our house, which was gifted to him by the Prophet ﷺ. Later, Abu Bakr provided me with a servant who took care of the horse. It was then that I had some relief.'

(BUKHARI, 'K. AL-NIKAH')

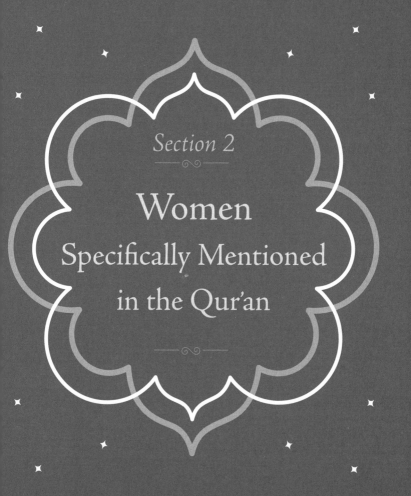

Section 2

Women
Specifically Mentioned
in the Qur'an

Believing Women
in the Qur'an

Apart from making numerous references to women in different contexts, the Qur'an portrays some women as role models. Below is their account, gleaned from the Qur'an and other authentic Islamic sources.

Maryam (Mary)

Maryam takes pride of place among all the women mentioned in the Quran; she is portrayed with these enviable appellations:

> Jesus's mother was a saintly woman.
>
> (AL-MA'IDA 5: 75)

> And recall when the angels told Mary: 'O Mary: Surely Allah has chosen you and cleansed you. He has preferred you to all the women in the world.'
>
> (AL 'IMRAN 3: 42)

She is prominent not only for being the mother of such an illustrious Messenger of Allah as Prophet

Jesus ﷺ, the Qur'an heaps praise on her for her piety,
her chastity and her devotion to Allah, as is evident
from the following Qur'anic description. It is notewor-
thy that Allah and His angels are found addressing her
directly. Her direct communion with Allah underscores her exalted status.

The reference to Mary giving birth to Prophet Jesus
ﷺ in a miraculous fashion is preceded by the Qur'anic description of Mary's own birth under special
circumstances; it shows Allah's close involvement in
Mary's life from the beginning:

> Recall when Imran's wife said: 'O my Lord, I ded-
> icate to You what is in my womb for Your service
> alone. So accept this from me. You are All Hear-
> ing, All Knowing.' When she gave birth to Mary,
> she said 'O my Lord, I have given birth to a female
> child… And a male is not like a female. I have
> named her Mary. I give her and her children in
> Your protection against the accursed Satan.' *Her
> Lord graciously accepted Mary, made her grow well
> and placed her under Zechariah's care.*
>
> (AL 'IMRAN 3: 35–37)

The italicised portion in the above Qur'anic passage
points unmistakably to Mary's special, exalted status
in the sight of Allah. That Allah accepted Mary for
His service, and arranged for her perfect upbringing
under Prophet Zechariah's care affirms her high

status. The Qur'an specifically mentions Mary's honour, glory and perfect growth in both physical and spiritual domains.

The special place enjoyed by her in the Divine scheme of things is evident from the following Qur'anic passage in which Allah's angels disclose to her how she will give birth to Prophet Jesus in a miraculous way:

> Recall when the angels said: 'O Mary, Allah gives you the good news of the word from Him. His name will be Christ Jesus, the son of Mary. He will be held in honour in this world and the Next. And He will be among those near Allah. He will speak to people, even though he will be in his cradle, and in his mature years. He will be in the company of the pious.'
>
> She said: 'How will I have a son when no man has ever touched me?' The angel said: 'Thus shall it be. God creates what He wills. When He decides something, He only says: "Be", and it is.'

(Al 'Imran 3: 45–47)

141

The above passage recounting Mary's direct interaction with the angels points also to her central role, both literally and figuratively, in the birth of an outstanding Messenger of Allah, Prophet Jesus ﷺ. She was entrusted with his miraculous birth, without the agency of a biological father.

Her giving birth to Prophet Jesus ﷺ is related in the

Qur'an at length:

Recite in this Book the account of Mary. She withdrew from her family to a place in the east (of Jerusalem). She placed a curtain, screening herself from people. God sent her His spirit which appeared before her as a human being in every respect. (Upon seeing him) she said: 'I take shelter from you with the Most Compassionate One, if you fear Allah.' He said: 'I am only a messenger from your Lord. I have come to you to give you a holy son.' She exclaimed: 'How can I have a son, when no man has ever touched me? I have never been unchaste.' He said: 'So it will be. Your Lord says that it is easy for Him. He will make him a sign for mankind. He will be mercy from Allah. This matter is already decided.'

She conceived him (Jesus) and retired with him to a far off place. The pains of childbirth took her to the trunk of a palm tree. She said: 'Ah! Would that I had died before this! Would that I had been forgotten!'

An angel announced to her from beneath (the palm tree): 'Do not be sad. Your Lord has provided a stream of water beneath you. Shake towards you the trunk of the palm tree. Fresh, ripe dates will fall upon you. Eat and drink, and cool your eyes. If you see anyone, tell him: "I have vowed a fast to the Most Compassionate One. So, I will not speak to anyone today."'

Then she brought the baby to her people, carrying him. They said: 'O Mary you have done something outrageous. O sister of Aaron, your father was

not an evil person. Nor was your mother unchaste.'
Upon this Maryam pointed to the child. They said:
'How can we talk to someone who is only a child,
lying in a cradle?'

However, the child cried out: 'I am a servant of
God. He has granted me the Book and made me a
Messenger.'

(MARYAM 19: 16–30)

This extensive account is reflective of Mary's excellence on the following counts:

- The Qur'an contains a detailed description of Mary, pointing as it does to her lofty status in the sight of Allah.
- Allah sent down to her His Spirit, which is the highest distinction imaginable for any human being, including the Messengers of Allah.
- Moreover, He sent that Spirit in the human form so as not to unsettle her. Although Mary was astonished at his appearance and argued with him cogently and on moral grounds, affirming her chastity, she was not panic-struck by the intrusion of a stranger into her privacy.
- She was given the glad tidings of the birth of an illustrious son who would be a sign and mercy from Allah for mankind until the end of time.
- Throughout the narrative, one notes the angels addressing her by name and conveying to her Allah's messages.

143

- Notwithstanding all the special arrangements about the announcement of the birth of a noble son to her, Mary, like any other woman, suffered from birth pangs. Moreover, she had to bear the brunt of her hostile community who charged her with having committed illicit sex. This physical and emotional ordeal tested her mettle further. Needless to add, she displayed utmost piety and self-surrender to Allah in all these trials and tribulations.

- Allah made special provision for her during the laborious birth; an angel directed her to draw upon the fresh dates and spring water made close at hand for her.

- Special arrangements were put in place in order to absolve her of the false charge of sexual misconduct hurled against her. The infant Jesus silenced her detractors, as he spoke in his cradle, affirming her chastity.

Little wonder then that in view of her many distinctions the Qur'an speaks highly of her along with some pious Messengers of Allah:

> Mention also the woman (Mary) who guarded her chastity. Allah breathed into her of His spirit. He made her and her son (Jesus) a sign for all people.
>
> (al-Anbiya' 21: 91)

Allah made Jesus the son of Mary and his mother
His signs. He gave them shelter on a high ground,
a peaceful place, with springs flowing in it.

(al-Mu'minun 23: 50)

To crown it all, the Qur'an presents Mary as a role
model while citing her outstanding traits: her protection of her chastity, her being a recipient of the
Divine spirit, her steadfastness and unshakable faith
in the face of ordeals and her subservience to Allah:

(Allah presents the example of) Mary, the daughter of Imran. She guarded her chastity. Allah
breathed into her body of His spirit. She testified
to words of her Lord and His Books. She was one
of the obedient (servants of Allah).

(al-Tahrim 66: 12)

145

Here are some more remarkable points about Mary
in the light of her description in the Qur'an and
Hadith:

- Like Prophet Jesus عليه السلام she is held in esteem to an
  equal degree by Muslims and Christians alike.
- According to a report narrated by Anas ibn Malik,
  she ranks among the four best women; the other three are the Pharaoh's believing wife, Asiya;
  Prophet Muhammad's first wife Khadijah, and his
  daughter, Fatimah.
- Surah 19 is named after her; she appears as a cen-

tral figure, not a peripheral one, in the account of
Prophet Jesus ﷺ, especially of his birth.

- In as many as sixteen instances the Qur'an refers to
  Jesus as the son of Mary. This highlights his special
  birth, without the usual agency of a father and the
  degree of respect that Allah placed upon her.

- Not only is Mary special, everyone around her is
  blessed with Allah's special favours. Her mother,
  Hannah receives Divine revelation, informing her
  of Allah's acceptance of her consecration. Prophet
  Zechariah ﷺ is amazed to note Mary getting a
  regular yet unusual supply of provisions inside her
  chamber:

  > Whenever Zechariah entered her chamber, he
  > found her provided with provision. He asked her:
  > 'Mary, how does this come to you?' She replied:
  > 'From Allah. Allah provides provision beyond
  > measure to whom He wills.'

  (AL 'IMRAN 3: 38)

Furthermore, Zechariah, Mary's guardian, was be-
stowed, with a son in his ripe, old age, though his wife
was barren.

- Allah accepted Mary for serving Him (AL 'IMRAN
  3: 37) notwithstanding her mother's gender-biased
  observation: 'O my Lord, I have given birth to a
  female child… And a male is not like a female.'
  (AL 'IMRAN 3: 36). Allah accepted Mary in view of
  her piety.

- She does not appear as a docile, timid young woman, ever ready to fall in line. On the contrary, as a discerning, intelligent girl she questions and argues with the angels and the Spirit who brought her the news of the virgin birth. Once she recognises it as a Divine command, she obeys and undergoes physical and psychological trauma while obeying the Divine command.

Queen of Sheba

Another woman receiving considerable attention in the Qur'an is the Queen of Sheba in Prophet Solomon's time.

Prophet Solomon ﷺ learns this about her from a hoopoe:

> 'I have brought for you a reliable report about Sheba. I found there a woman ruling over them and she has all things. She has a mighty throne. I saw her and her people prostrating before the sun, rather than Allah…'

Solomon said: 'We will soon find out whether you speak the truth or are a liar. Take my letter and deliver it to them. Then draw back from them and see what answer they give.'

The Queen said: 'O my chiefs, a letter worthy of respect has been delivered to me. It is from Solomon and it reads: "In the name of Allah, Most Compassionate, Most Merciful. Do not be arrogant against me but come to me in submission."'

She continued: 'O chiefs, advise me on this matter. I do not decide any affair without you…' She said: 'As kings enter a country (as conquerors), they spoil it and disgrace the nobles there. This is how they behave. I will send them a gift and see what response my envoys get.'… Solomon directed that her throne (which he had procured) be altered in order to find out whether she recognises it or is she one of those who are not directed to the truth. When she arrived, she was asked: 'Is this your throne?' She replied: 'It is just like this.' … She exclaimed: 'O my Lord! I wronged my soul. Now, with Solomon, I surrender myself to Allah, the Lord of the universe.'

(AL-NAML 27: 22, 27–32, 34–35, 41-42, 44).

The Queen of Sheba emerges as a sagacious, intelligent woman, adept at diplomacy and political strategies. On receiving Prophet Solomon's letter she takes her chiefs into confidence. Her move of sending a gift in order to evaluate Prophet Solomon's character and conduct underscores her wisdom. More importantly, she responds to the call of truth positively and immediately. In no time she admits her error and embraces true faith. Her high social stature did not blind her to truth. Like Mary, she is a pious, mature and discerning female, wedded essentially to the cause of truth. She takes bold and sound initiatives and exercises her power judiciously.

Pharaoh's Believing Wife

She stands out for her enviable commitment to truth, even at the risk of losing her position and possessions, and facing persecution. She accepted belief in the One True God, though she was the wife of Pharaoh, a die-hard unbeliever who laid claim to divinity. Although she was surrounded by those given to eliminating truth at all costs, she perceived truth and readily accepted it. Accordingly, a glowing tribute is paid to her in the Qur'an:

> Allah presents before the believers the example of the wife of Pharaoh. She prayed: 'O my Lord, build for me a house near You in Paradise. Deliver me from Pharaoh and his evil actions, and the wrong doing people.'
>
> (AL-TAHRIM 66: 11)

150

The Qur'an portrays her as a role model in recognition of her commitment, courage and strong faith even in the face of adverse and hostile surroundings.

Prophet Moses's Mother

Like Mary, Prophet Moses's mother holds the distinction of having received Divine directives. She is applauded for her self-restraint and perseverance. As in the case of Mary, Allah rescued her too when she faced persecution.

Pharaoh claimed to be a god, yet he feared being overthrown at the hands of the Israelites, and therefore ordered that all the newborn Israelite boys be put to death while girls be spared. The latter were to serve as maids for the ruling class. The Israelites being a religious minority group, were helpless victims of Pharaoh's oppression. It was against this historical backdrop that Allah devised their liberation under the leadership of Prophet Moses ﷺ. Like other Israelite infants, the baby Moses was liable to be killed at birth. At that point Allah confided in Moses's mother, who played a pivotal role in Moses's survival which, in turn, led to the downfall of Pharaoh and the liberation of the Israelites:

151

> Allah inspired Moses's mother: 'Suckle your child. However, when you fear for his life, cast him into the river. Do not fear or grieve. We will restore him to you and appoint him one of Our Messengers.'
>
> Accordingly, Pharaoh's men picked him up (i.e. Moses from the river) so that he may be an enemy and a cause of distress to them… Pharaoh's wife exclaimed: 'This child is a joy for our eyes. Do not kill

him. He may benefit us or we may adopt him as a son.' They did not realise (what they were doing).

The heart of Moses's mother felt restless. Had Allah not strengthened her heart as a firm believer, she would have disclosed the secret (about Moses).

She asked Moses's sister to look for him. She kept watching him while they (Pharaoh's men) did not notice this. Allah decreed that Moses refuse the breast of nurses. It was then that Moses's sister told them: 'May I direct you to the members of a household who will bring up the child for you with sincerity?'

Thus Allah restored Moses to her mother that her eyes may be comforted and she may not grieve any longer. She thus realised that Allah's promise is true. However, most of the people do not understand this.

(AL-QASAS 28: 7–12)

152

Notwithstanding her maternal love which prompted her restlessness, Moses's mother acted in accordance with the Divine plan. Allah rewarded her for her patience as He restored the baby Moses to her. For so doing, He devised a strategy in which Moses's sister also played an important role. Her loss of and ultimate reunion with her son brings to mind another moving Qur'anic narrative of almost the same import: the young Joseph's disappearance, his father Jacob's sorrow and grief and finally their reunion, facilitated by Allah. Moses's mother typifies maternal love and more importantly, patience and endurance for the sake of Allah.

Prophet Shuayb's Daughters

In their encounter with Prophet Moses ﷺ Prophet Shuayb's two daughters strike us as intelligent, modest and resourceful young women. Also, they appear as dutiful daughters, shouldering the responsibility which their old father was unable to perform. The Qur'anic account is as follows:

> When Moses reached the watering place in Midian, he saw a crowd watering (their flock). He spotted there two women besides them, holding back their flock. He asked them: 'What is the matter with you?' They replied: 'We cannot water our flock until these shepherds take away their flocks. Our father is a very old man.' Moses watered their flock … After a while one of the two women came to him, walking with modesty. She told him: 'My father has invited you in order to reward you for having watered our flock.'… Then one of the two women said: 'O father, engage him on wages. The best of men to employ is he who is strong and trustworthy.'
>
> (al-Qasas 28: 23–26)

153

The daughters of Prophet Shuayb did not mingle in the crowd with the shepherds but waited for their turn; they walked modestly when they approached Moses. This points to their excellent character and conduct. At the same time, they confidently and pragmatically advised their father to hire the young Moses whom they discerningly described as a strong, reliable person. Eventually their father gave one of them in marriage to Moses.

Allah's Response to Some Women's Pleas

The Qur'an depicts Allah responding positively to the pleas of several women in need.

Allah's grace blessed two barren women, the wives of Prophets Zechariah and Abraham 🕊. Allah granted them sons in their old age.

Surah al-Mujadilah opens with the complaint lodged by Khawlah bint Thalabah and Allah's instant redressal of her grievance. Her husband had pronounced *zihar*, a pre-Islamic, *Jahiliyah* form of severing the marital tie. In response to her plea for relief, Allah forbade this loathsome practice once and for all:

> (O Prophet), Allah heard the statement of the woman who argued with you about her husband. She appealed to Allah…
>
> Those among you who divorce their wives by *zihar* (declaring their wives to be their mothers) should realise that they are not their mothers. Their mothers are those who gave birth to them. Those who pronounce *zihar* say something dishonourable and false.
>
> (al-Mujadilah 58: 1-2)

By forbidding this abominable practice of *zihar* Islam challenged an established custom of the time that was grossly unfair towards women.

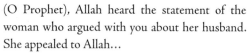

Gender parity characterises many Islamic commands and practices: In *lian* (husband's accusation of infidelity against his wife), *tahkim* (marital dispute arbitration) and right to inheritance, women enjoy parity with men.

Disbelieving Women in the Qur'an

In sharp contrast to the aforementioned pious women, the Qur'an also mentions some wicked ones. Despite their marital tie with such illustrious Messengers of Allah as Prophets Noah عَلَيْهِ السَّلَام and Lot عَلَيْهِ السَّلَام their wives are censured for their lack of faith. Even their close association with their Prophet husbands could not instil true faith into them. The Qur'an reproaches them for their treachery:

> Allah presents for the unbelievers the example of the wives of Noah and Lot. They were married to two pious servants of Allah. However, they were false to their husbands. Their husbands could not help them against Allah. These two women were told: 'Enter the Hellfire along with others who enter it.'
>
> (al-Tahrim 66: 10)

Potiphar's wife

In the context of Prophet Joseph's account, the Egyptian Potiphar's wife, known as Zulaykhah in popular lore, appears as a temptress. She personifies *nafs* (the base self), keen on gratifying desire, without any regard for any moral values. She seduces the young Joseph, who was under her care in her house. Shamelessly she asks Joseph to have sex with her:

> But she, in whose house Joseph was staying, tried to seduce him. She closed the doors and said: 'Come on now.' He replied: 'God forbid, your husband is my master. He has taken good care of me. The wrongdoers never prosper.'
>
> She, however, advanced towards him. Had Joseph not seen the sign of His Lord, he too, would have advanced towards her. This is how Allah saved him from evil and a shameful action.
>
> (Yusuf 12: 23–24)

Worse, she levelled the charge of sexual misconduct against Joseph. Unabashedly she paraded the exceptionally beautiful and handsome Joseph before some Egyptian ladies in order to justify her infatuation for him. Her lack of remorse and moral fibre comes out in the following Qur'anic passage:

> Some women in the town began saying: 'Potiphar's wife is trying to seduce her slave. She is in passionate love with him. We think she has gone too far

into error.' When she heard of their gossip, she invited them to a party. She gave each of them a knife. (While they were cutting and eating fruits), she said to Joseph: 'Come before them.' When they saw him, they were so carried away that they cut their hands. They exclaimed: 'How perfect is God! This Joseph is not a human being. He is no one but a noble angel.'

(It was then that) she said: 'This is the one about whom you blame me. I did try to seduce him. But he held back. If he does not do what I wish him to, he will be certainly put into prison and humiliated.'

(YUSUF 12: 30–32)

However, her ruse was soon exposed. Everyone acclaimed Joseph's integrity and chastity as he stood exonerated from the charge levelled by her. Eventually she publicly acknowledged the smokescreen fabricated by her:

The king asked the women: 'What happened when you tried to seduce Joseph?' They replied: 'God forbid! We did not find any evil in him.'

Potiphar's wife confessed: 'Now the truth has come to light. It was I who had tried to seduce him. He is true and innocent.'

(YUSUF 12: 51)

Abu Lahab's wife

Abu Lahab was Prophet Muhammad's uncle. However, both he and his wife were die-hard unbelievers and inveterate enemies of the Prophet (peace be upon him). His wife did all that she could to torment the Prophet (peace be upon him) by way of piling up rubbish or thorns in his way. Abu Lahab and his wife are among those few unbelievers whom the Qur'an reproaches by name and declares Hell as their abode:

> Abu Lahab's power will be destroyed. He stands condemned. All his gains and his wealth will not help him. He will burn soon in the flaming Hell-fire, along with his wife, who will carry wood as fuel. She will have a rope of rough palm leaves around her neck.
>
> (AL-LAHAB III: 1–15)

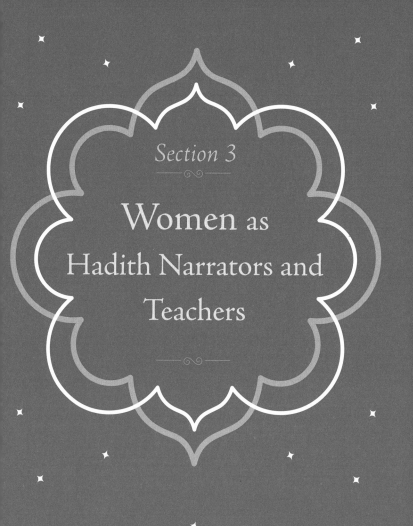

Section 3

Women as
Hadith Narrators and
Teachers

Some of the eminent Companions who have narrated Hadith on the authority of Aishah include:

- Abu Bakr
- Umar ibn al-Khattab
- Abu Hurayrah
- Abu Musa al-Ashari
- Abdullah ibn Abbas
- Abdullah ibn Umar
- Amr ibn al-Aas

(AL-MUHADDITHAT)[1]

---

1. M. Akram Nadvi, *al-Muhaddithat*: The Women Scholars in Islam. Oxford, Interface Publications, 2007.

Among those who have narrated Hadith on the authority of the Prophet's wife, Umm Salmah are:

- Masruq
- Urwah ibn Zubayr
- Ata ibn Abi Rabah
- Ata ibn Yasar
- Ikrimah
- Abdullah ibn Abbas
- Said ibn al-Musayyab

(AL-MUHADDITHAT)

161

The following have narrated Hadith on the authority of the Prophet's wife, Hafsah:

- Harithah ibn Wahb
- Abdullah ibn Umar
- Abd al-Rahman ibn Harith
- Abu Bakr ibn Sulayman

(AL-MUHADDITHAT)

The following Lady Companions are some other sources of Hadith reports:

- Maymunah
- Durah bint Abi Lahab
- Khawlah bint Hakim
- Rayidah bint Karamah
- Amrah bint Abd al-Rahman
- Fatimah al-Khuzaiyyah
- Hind bint Harith
- Umm Abdullah al-Dawsiyya
- Aishah bint Arjad
- Aishah bint Saad ibn Abi Waqqas
- Asma bint Yazid
- Asma bint Umays

(AL-MUHADDITHAT)

Hafiz ibn Asakir (d. 571 H) has cited Hadith reports from eighty women.

(AL-MUHADDITHAT)

Abu Saad al-Sama'ni (d. 562 H) has authored an account of sixty-nine female Hadith narrators.

(AL-MUHADDITHAT)

———— ⟡ ————

As many as 2764 Hadith feature in the six standard collections of Hadith on the authority of lady Companions.

More importantly, the Hadith narrated by them are not restricted to the personal hygiene and purification of women. They embrace a wide range of topics including prayer, fasting, Zakah, Hajj, food, clothing, business, jihad, marriage and divorce, death, the Hereafter, supplications, morals and manners and the Prophet's illustrious life.

(AL-MUHADDITHAT)

———— ⟡ ————

Some Hadith are on the authority of only the lady Companions and have served as the basis of legal rulings inferred from them. Take as illustrative the Hadith related by Barirah, a slave girl who was set free by Aishah. According to Ibn Hajar al-Asqalani, 'Some Imams have collected the useful points of this Hadith, which are more than three hundred. I have summarised these in my book, *Fath al-Bari*.'

(Al-Muhaddithat)

The Hadith narrated by Subay'ah al-Aslamiyyah, on the waiting period to be observed by a widow, by Busrah bint Safwan on ablution, and by Umm Atiyyah on the washing of the deceased are crucial to the legal rulings on these issues. This underscores the lady Companions' substantial contribution to *fiqh* (jurisprudence).

(Al-Muhaddithat)

Karimah al-Marwaziyyah (d. 461 H) stands out as an eminent teacher of *Sahih Bukhari*; Al-Khatib al-Baghdadi, a distinguished Hadith scholar and historian was her student.

(Al-Muhaddithat)

Aishah bint Muhammad ibn Abd al-Hadi al-Maqdisiyyah taught *Sahih Bukhari*. Among her disciples are such famous scholars as Ibn Hajar, Hafiz al-Dimashqi and Taqi al-Din al-Fasi.

(Al-Muhaddithat)

Umm al-Khayr Fatimah bint Abi al-Hasan Ali (d. 532 H) won wide acclaim as a teacher of *Sahih Muslim*, a major, authentic Hadith collection.

Zaynab bint Umar ibn Kindi (d. 699 H) also attained fame as a popular teacher of *Sahih Muslim*. Some other notable lady teachers were Safiah bint Ahmad ibn Qudamah (d. 714 H) and Aishah bint Muhammad ibn Abd al-Hadi (d. 816 H).

(Al-Muhaddithat)

Khadijah bint 'Abd al-Hamid (d. 734) excelled as a teacher of an important Hadith collection, *Jami 'Tirmidhi*.

(Al-Muhaddithat)

The *Musnad* of Ahmad ibn Hanbal contains 2405 Hadith narrated by Aishah. *Al-Istiab li ma Istadrakthu Aishah al-Ashab* carries Aishah's critique on Hadith reports and opinions of Companions. Abu Mansur and al-Muhsin ibn Muhammad (d. 489 H) has compiled this work.

⸻ ◌ ⸻

Jalal al-Din al-Suyuti has compiled and edited all the Hadith narrated by Fatimah, entitled *Musnad Fatimah.*

⸻ ◌ ⸻

Juz Biba is a collection of Hadith related to Umm Izza Biba bint 'Abd al-Samad (d. 474 H).

⸻ ◌ ⸻

Mashyakhah Shuhdah by Shuhdah bint Abi Nasr (d. 574 H) contains 114 Hadith, compiled by her student, Abd al-Aziz ibn Mahmud.

⸻ ◌ ⸻

Mashyakhah Khadijah is a collection of Hadith related to Khadijah bint al-Qadi (d. 618 H).

———— ⬥ ————

Abu Abdullah al-Birzah has compiled *Mashyakhah Karimah*, with regards to the Syrian scholar, Umm al-Fadl Karimah bint Abi Muhammed (d. 641 H).

(AL-MUHADDITHAT)

———— ⬥ ————

Some other leading women Hadith narrators include:

Successors
- Amrah bint Abd al-Rahman
- Hafsah bint Sirin
- Umm al-Darda

2nd Century Hijri Hadith Scholars
- Umm al-Aswad al-Khuzaiyyah
- Ubaydah bint Nabil al-Hijaziyyah
- Munyah bint Ubayd al-Asalamiyyah
- Umm Nailah al-Khuzaiyyah
- Aishah bint Sad ibn Abi Waqqas
- Fatimah bint Jafar ibn Muhammad al-Sadiq

(AL-MUHADDITHAT)

Index of Qur'anic Passages

171

Subject Index

172

174

176